By Zippora Karz

THE SUGARLESS PLUM - A ballerina's triumph over diabetes

BALLERINA DREAMS
A book for Children with Diabetes

By Zippora Karz

Illustrations and page design by
Jenne van Eeghen

The material contained in this book
is not intended as a substitute for medical advice
nor is it intended to diagnose, treat, cure, or prevent disease.
If you have a medical issue or illness, consult a qualified physician.

A Zippy Book™
Published by Zippy Books Publishing

Copyright © 2007 - 2013 Zippora Karz

Illustrations by Jenne van Eeghen
Cover Illustration by Jenne van Eeghen
Zippy Books logo photo by Paul Kolnik
Interior book design by Jenne van Eeghen
Printed in the United States of America

ISBN - 13: 978 - 0615903187
ISBN - 10: 0615903185

All rights reserved. No part of this book may be reproduced or transmitted in any form or by any means, electronic or mechanical, including photocopying, recording, or by any information storage and retrieval system, without the prior written permission from the Publisher.

This publication is designed to provide accurate and authoritative information in regard to the subject matter covered. It is sold on the understanding that the Publisher is not engaged in rendering professional services. If professional advice or other expert assistance is required, the services of a competent professional should be sought.

To my grandmother Gloria and my mother Ellen
for the gift of dance and making dreams real.

To my teacher Sheila for the joy of dance that is ballet.

To my sister Romy for being by my side through it all, even writing this book.

And to Julie Mettenberg for the wonderful editing.

A very special thank you to Dr. Fran Kaufman
for her contribution both to this book and to the world.

On any other night Zippy would have
begged for a bedtime story,
but tonight was different.
All Zippy wanted to think of was how
wonderful this day had been -
her first day of ballet.

Zippy loved the feel of the ballet barre in the palm of her hand as she held it tightly, determined to stand with her toes pointing out while her heels touched.
This was first position.

It wasn't easy, especially to keep her head and chest up at the same time, but by the end of the class she began to feel graceful and elegant.

That evening she danced around the living room and right into bed with her slippers still on her feet.

Zippy felt so free when she danced, she wanted to dance all the time.

She worked hard, and every day she got better. Soon she was turning and jumping and dancing on her pointes.

Then, one day, Zippy's teacher asked to speak to her after class.

She told Zippy she had noticed how hard Zippy had been working, and how much she had improved. "We are going to have a special performance," she said. "I want you to be the leading ballerina."

The leading ballerina! Zippy was ecstatic.

Rehearsals began the following week. There was a solo dance, and a dance with her prince. She couldn't wait to be lifted high in the air.

A few weeks of rehearsals went by, and though Zippy was loving her role, something was bothering her. Strange things had begun to happen to her body. First, she was always going to the bathroom. She was always hungry and thirsty, even after she had a lot to eat and drink.

Then, one day in rehearsal, in the middle of her solo, Zippy's head felt foggy and her legs began to shake. Before she knew it, she was on the floor. She had fallen down.

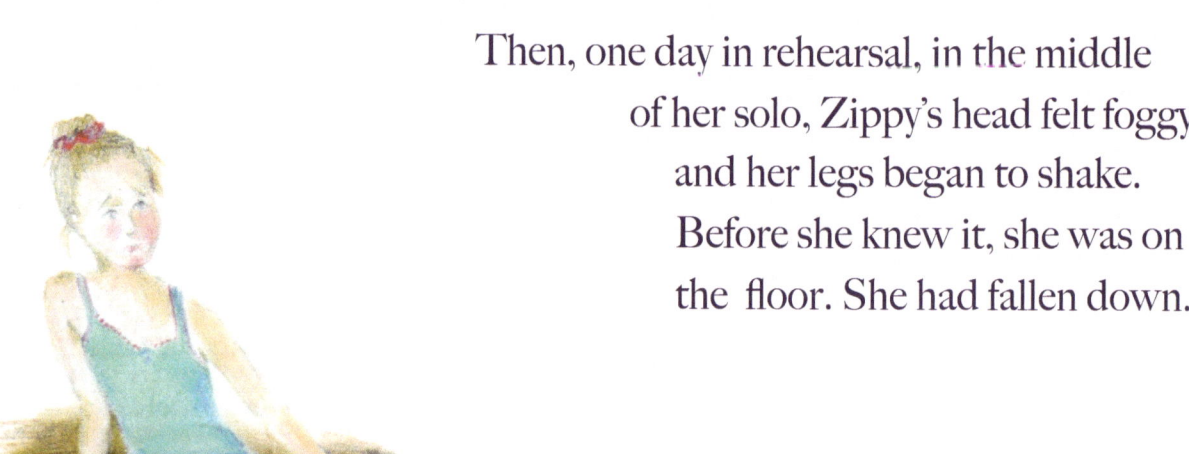

Zippy thought she was just tired from rehearsing so much for the performance, but her mom and dad took her to the doctor anyway.

"I am sorry," the doctor told them, " but Zippy's symptoms are being caused by a disease called diabetes. Her kind of diabetes is called type 1."

They all sat silent, shocked and worried.

"Diabetes isn't easy to explain," the doctor continued.
"It involves a chemical in the blood called insulin. When we eat, food is broken down into sugar. This sugar is what will feed the cells of the body, from our eyes to our toes, so they can work properly. But something has to help get the sugar from the blood into the cells. Insulin is like a key that unlocks a door; it is what opens the cell up so the sugar can get in.
Some bodies, like Zippy's, have problems making insulin, so they do not have enough."

"What can we do?" asked Zippy's father anxiously. The doctor smiled and told them not to worry. "Although we cannot fix Zippy's body so it will make insulin, we can come close," he said. "Zippy will have to take shots of insulin every day and she will need to test her blood sugar levels to make sure she takes the right amount. Eating foods that are healthy will help - and exercise is very important."

Exercise! Zippy remembered her dancing. She wanted to know about the shots but first she had to know if she could still perform.
"Will I be able to dance?" she nervously asked.
The doctor thought a moment. "Of course you can. Dancing has taught you how to balance on one leg. Now you will need to learn how to balance other things like food and your activity with your insulin levels. The problem is that when you take insulin and are very active your blood sugar level could drop too low. Whenever you dance, and especially when you perform, you must promise to check your blood sugar levels.

If you are too low you must have something sweet like sugar or juice. So always keep some sugar off-stage, just in case your blood sugar drops too low. It will not be easy. But being a ballerina isn't easy. It will take a lot of discipline, but I know you can do it."

Zippy didn't care what it would take. If it meant she could still dance and perform, she would do it.

It took her a few weeks to get the hang of her new routine.
She tested her own blood sugar by pricking her finger and squeezing out a tiny drop of blood for the monitor. She took shots with no complaints.
She even made sure not to eat unhealthy foods.
And not a moment went by when she did not dream of getting back to rehearsals and preparing for her performance.

Finally, the doctor said okay: she could return to rehearsals.
Eagerly, Zippy went to the studio. As she approached the door she could hear the music for her solo. But when she entered the studio, excited to be back, she stopped suddenly.
She could not believe what she saw.

Another girl was dancing her solo!

Zippy was devastated. She had been replaced.

The teacher tried to explain. "When you were first diagnosed you seemed so tired and weak. And then we didn't see you for many weeks now, while you were gone the rehearsals had to go on. Zippy, maybe it would be best if you didn't pressure yourself right now. There will be other performances in the future. I'm very sorry."

Zippy cried all night long. She understood why the teacher had replaced her. She had not danced since starting her insulin shots, and she felt nervous about it herself. But she had to try - she had to have the chance. She had to dance!

Zippy's tears turned to anger. "Why is this happening to me?" she cried to her mother. "It just isn't fair!"

That night, Zippy cried herself into a deep sleep.

She dreamt she was a ballerina about to perform on a brightly lit stage. As the music began, she could feel every note in the cells of her body. Her heart welled with excitement. She took off in a dance of joy and freedom, jumping and turning across the stage. Her arms moved up and down like a swan, soft and graceful. Her legs were as strong as a cheetah's. She never wanted this dance to end.

Suddenly, everything came to a stop. There, in front of her, stood the most beautiful ballerina Zippy had ever seen. She wore a flowing dress that was every color of the rainbow, and she held a sparkling wand in her hand.

She spoke softly and wisely. "I am here to remind you what you already know in your heart. Remember this feeling. It is the power of your passion. Believe in it, trust in it, do not give up on it. It is your strength."

With that, she disappeared.

When Zippy awoke the next morning, the words echoed in her head and her heart. "Trust in it. Do not give up on it. It is your strength." Dancing was her passion. Zippy promised herself she would not give up.

Zippy went to the rehearsal and asked the teacher to give her another chance. She told her she would check her blood sugar before she performed, and she would always have sugar nearby.

The teacher was still unsure but decided to let Zippy try at the rehearsal.

Zippy checked her blood sugar level and put her sugar nearby. She took a deep breath and looked at all the silent faces curious to see what was going to happen. She took her place to begin her solo.

Zippy began to dance, and dance did she ever! Zippy was bursting with strength and passion and danced better than before. She had proven to herself and to her teacher that diabetes would not stop her dancing.

The teacher gladly gave her part pack. Even the other girl was happy to let Zippy have her part back.

At last the day had come.

Zippy felt like a princess as she prepared for the performance. She powdered her face, blushed her cheeks and glossed her lips. She stepped into her pink tutu and pinned a tiara of diamonds and pearls upon her head. She laced up her toe shoes and warmed up her muscles.

She made sure to check her blood sugar level with her monitor and placed her sugar behind a curtain just off-stage. Everything was set.

Then the stage manager called "places everyone!" Zippy stepped center stage. She took a deep breath. She thought about everything she had been through: finding out she had diabetes, all of her doubts and fears, and almost giving up.

Then she remembered her dream. Here she was. She had believed in her passion and let it give her the strength to make her dream come true.

Her radiant face glowed even brighter.

As the curtain rose she could feel the warmth of the lights on her body. Calm washed over her as the music began. Her heart and body could not wait to dance.

Zippy had never danced before as she did that day. She was magnificent.

As soon as the curtain came down, Zippy knew she would dance many more performances. She would always check her blood sugar beforehand, and she would always carefully place some sugar close by, just off - stage.

Most of all, Zippy would always dance from
the passion she felt in her heart that day.
She knew it would give her the strength
to succeed despite any challenge,
on-stage and off.

Diabetes explained

Diabetes can strike at any age. The diagnosis of diabetes is made when a significant increase in the concentration of glucose, a form of sugar, is found in the blood because it can't be processed normally. Glucose is what fuels our every move and our every thought. The glucose we need comes from the food we eat. But our body can't use it without insulin, a hormone produced by the pancreas.

In diabetes, insulin can't play its proper role because it is either present in insufficient amounts or the body's cells are resistant to it.

Diabetes takes two main forms. In type 1, the immune system destroys the cells in the pancreas that produce insulin. Type 1 diabetes typically appears in childhood and progresses rapidly. Ninety percent of people with diabetes have the other kind, which is known as type 2. In type 2 diabetes, the pancreas makes insulin, but the body's cells don't respond normally to it.

As with type 1, the cells go hungry while, paradoxically, glucose accumulates in the blood.

The classic signs and symptoms of diabetes are excess thirst and urination, hunger, weight loss, fatigue, and slower healing of sores. In type 1, these symptoms seem to come on abruptly. But the signs of type 2 diabetes can be more subtle, so subtle in fact that almost a third of those with the disease have no idea they have diabetes.

Throughout the world, there has been an increase in efforts designed to find the cure for diabetes and ways to prevent it. While researchers work hard in these areas, doctors and other health care providers are making breakthroughs in better ways to treat diabetes and support those touched by this disease.

Francine Kaufman
Distinguished Professor Emeritus of Pediatrics
USC School of Medicine

About the Author

ZIPPORA KARZ, former soloist with the New York City Ballet, danced with the company from 1983 - 1999. She now serves as a teacher and repetiteur for the George Balanchine Trust, rehearsing and staging Balanchine's choreography for a host of national and international dance companies. She is also a diabetes spokesperson and educator who regularly addresses major diabetes conferences and organizations worldwide. She lives in Los Angeles, California.
Visit her Web site at www.ZipporaKarz.com

www.ingramcontent.com/pod-product-compliance
Lightning Source LLC
LaVergne TN
LVHW072116070426
835510LV00002B/86